Logos
and other logoi

poems by George J. Dance

Principled Press
Toronto, Ontario, Canada

Lulu Press
Baltimore, MD, USA

Logos, and other logoi: poems by George J. Dance

Printed by Lulu Press for Principled Press.

ISBN 978-0-9948600-2-6

An earlier version of "Logos" was published in *Freedom's Child* 2:1 (June 1982).
"Away," " September Night," "Ideas of March," and "Prey" were published in *Other Voices International* 42 (2008).
"Demiurges," "A Scroll," and "Threnody" were published in *The HorrorZine*, Spring 2015.
"Demons" was published in *The Horror Zine*, Spring 2020.

First edition November 2021

Printed in U.S.A.

Logos
and other logoi

Contents

September

Can I touch you in autumn,
beautiful soft-skinned one
fragrant with heady wishes?

by *Vizant d'Or*
translated by George J. Dance

Premonition

The sun has never seemed so warm and bright,
The grass and trees have never looked as green
As in this calm September morning light,
But something else is with me, though unseen:
A polar wind that blows by, harsh and keen,
And leaves me feeling numbed, alone, and ill
As I envision what that gust will mean:
Green leaves and grass to wither in its chill,
Gray snow to bury all, black ice to freeze the kill.

Autumn Leaving

The beasts, and even bugs
are sleeping now.
Again the leaves are turning
both golden and bloody
in a celebration of life
before they die and fall to rest
beneath a bone-grey shroud.
The birds are gone now
searching for summer;
how lucky the birds, to fly away
and still be together.
I, too, have flown
but alone, and not far enough
for autumn has caught me
and holds me pinned, inert
in its soporific wind
with summer and home both so far away.

Away

Away again, I'm missing you
And when I'll see you, I don't know.
I really don't know what to do.

I seem to see you for a few
Mere seconds, but then – poof! – you blow
Away again. I'm missing you.

Another night I must get through.
My thoughts meander to and fro.
I really don't know what to do.

I doodle or I write haiku,
Prosaic scraps I have to throw
Away again. I'm missing you.

I could watch "Captain Kangaroo"
Or "Friends," or "Simpsons," or – oh no,
I really *don't* know what to do!

I need to stay alive for you,
Come back to you, and never go
Away. Again, I'm missing you.
I really don't know what to do.

Deer

A quiver of wind, a glint of sun
unmoving, tensed as if to run
a flickering flame trembling
an infinitely gentle thing.

Aim the gun – squeeze
see my own blood gush
from the open wound.

The Key

There is a killer, screaming to get out;
He beats his bars and rants till short of breath.
I block my ears, but still can hear him shout
Of bloody violence, destruction, death.
I must keep him confined inside of me;
I am the only one who holds the key.

There is another man locked up in there
Though quietly he mourns on his sad fate,
On wisdom and on beauty he would share
But keeps within his cell until too late.
Before I die, I must set that man free;
I am the only one who holds the key.

September Night

Silence
and a deeper silence
when the crickets
hesitate
      - Summer Haiku, Leonard Cohen

Around the campfire
smell of burning
leaves in
silence.

Crickets serenade
to soothe
the circling dark.
And a deeper silence

swoops down after
a muted splash
quiets the band,
when the crickets

pause – for an instant
nothing rings out like a gong,
for an instant our heartbeats
hesitate.

October

How soon leaves fall
green   canary   brown
scattered alike on the ground

Demiurges

But demiurges are around,
Angels, demons, too, they say
Jinns and trolls and dwarves and fay
(Though no one ever hears a sound
And not one footprint has been found)
These things are all surrounding me
Commanding me, controlling me
And this is not mere fantasy
Insanity, or LSD
But virtual reality.

The Dwarf beneath the Bed

Lie back and close your eyes, my babe,
    Lay down your weary head,
And please try not to think about
    The dwarf beneath the bed.

An evil, cruel, misshapen dwarf
    Lives right here in your room.
He's hiding in the furthest cracks,
    And muttering in the gloom:

He hates the light, he hates the truth,
    He hates the whole world, too;
The one thing that he hates the most
    Is pretty babes like you.

He wants to kill us all, my dear,
    Because he hates us so.
Tonight he might just cut your throat
    And you will never know;

Mama and I will be asleep
    So there will be no hearer
If Dwarfie parts your jugular
    With fragments of your mirror.

Now go to sleep, my darling; please
    Forget what I have said.
Pray God you do not think about
    The dwarf before you're dead!

That Gopher

I saw that gopher in the garden again, so I got my gun and it too, but then I thought, hey, what if it's not dead, so I told the boy to take the sledge and bash its head in. He whined a bit – never killed nothing before – but he knew better so he went. I watched from behind the glass as he dragged his ass out there, slow like he was going to a whipping. Then he just stood there for the longest time, just staring at it, till I raised the window and yelled. Then real slow he took up that sledge, and hit, and took it up again and hit, and hit, and hit again, and again, and I screamed at him that's enough, it's dead, but he hit again and again and again, hammer head splashing in the pulp, and again, and I had to go out and pull that crazy kid off.

On Galveston Island

A found poem

from a letter to the editor
Galveston County Daily News:

In the past year
there have been three
heinous stories
of visitors
to Galveston Island
being charged
with torturing
or murdering
their innocent children
and in two of the cases,
leaving them, like trash,
to be picked up.

People who have
no respect
for human life
need to be punished
severely
for their crimes.

I also ask visitors
and residents

to be more conscientious
about their rubbish.

There are trash receptacles
all over the island.
There is no excuse
for this place
to look like a pigsty.

My Father's House

This is my father's house, although
The man died thirteen years ago.
They said it would be quite all right
To take a drive to see it now.

Dad laid those grey foundation blocks
And built the whole thing (from a box),
Toiling after each full day's work.
I helped, though I was only six.

Look, here's the back door I would use
And here's where I'd remove my shoes
To enter; there I'd leave my things
And, when allowed, climb up these stairs.

In this room I'd wash many a dish,
Gaze out this window, and I'd wish
To be so many other places.
(Wishy-washy? Oh, I guess!)

Outside, the garden that he grew
Where I would work the summers through,
While watching my friends run and play
Mysterious games I never knew.

That room's all changed; oh, where is it,
The one chair I was let to sit?
(For boys can be such filthy things.)
Which, the corner where boys were put?

Oh ... down that hall there is a room
Where I'd be shut (as in a tomb)
After the meal, to make no noise,
To read or play alone, and then

Lights out: in bed by nine each night,
Some nights wanting to pee with fright,
Face and pyjama bottoms down
As for my father's belt I'd wait.

Oh, if I were a millionaire
I'd buy my father's house, and there
I'd build a bonfire, oh so high
Its flames would light up all the air.

Demons

We'd dress as ghosts or devils once a year
to run and yell like vandals home-to-home,
high on the sugar we'd take by threats of harm
we'd chant at every door – but there was no fear
for we played at roles from long-forgotten darks
when noxious flesh-bound demons stalked, who'd kill
or maim at whim; those who'd evade their rule
confined like sheep, asleep behind bars and locks.

My children's children dress and do the like
but chaperoned (kids don't go out alone)
and only in the twilight; when it's night,
parent and child are locked within the home
because "It's just not safe these days" – a fact
so calmly noted: Demon time is back.

November

dying land
   crying sky
      cold, cold tears

Autumn Music

When days grow bored
with summer hues,
embracing brown
and turbid grey,
then look for love
in fallen leaves
for love too often
falls
that
way.

18

Night (Fall)

The grass shone emerald in the morning light
But fades to grey now as the autumn moon
Glints off the darkened waters in the bight,
A stray reflection of some lost balloon.
The trees that I remember as so bright
(Persimmon, scarlet, orange, gold) at noon
Have dulled to tarry black and ghostly white
While round them heaps of curled grey ash are
strewn.
So all has faded that was my delight
In early hours; now, sounds are out of tune,
Shades blur, words slur, once-dear beliefs are trite,
And everything that lives must die too soon.
    Nothing besides remains within my sight
    but these few pale reflections in the night.

Faces

Faces colored with calm
Concealing pain,
Inside shattered with turmoil,
Outside so placid and plain:
Who taught you to hide behind walls
And behind shields
To trick us?
Who do you fear?
That face is a fake:
A dark, wooden mask
That hides you in shadow.
Who are you?
Why are you afraid to show me?
Why do you want to look like another face?
That face is evil.
Kill the face.
Can you?
Can you show me your self,
Let me see the turmoil in you,
Please?
Be brave!
Kill that ugly face.

by bhawani and George J. Dance

20

A Scroll

By the river I saw geese fly
Like black angels, far and high.
Trees were cracks in a scarlet sky,
A scent of smoke, a dolorous cry:

> "Fallen is Babylon the Great,"
> Cries the wild goose to his mate.
> "All for fires to consume.
> Ashes, ashes for their doom."

> "Still we learned to love their land,"
> Softer now she answers, "and
> Safely in the south land, we
> Will miss their insecurity."

On the banks red sumac lay,
Fires banked at close of day.
Will I watch those fires burn?
Will I see the geese return?

Remembrance

Man has but to raise
His arms, and there is a cross.
How could we forget?

Cease Fire

For one full day we got to stop the business
Of trying to kill each other. We could stand,
And leave the trench, and meet in no-man's-land
To wish the other side a Merry Christmas.

One Hun pulled out a flask, gave me a drink –
I shared my smokes – we played a few card tricks,
Then showed our wives' and kids' and girly pics,
Said "Aww..." and did the old nudge-nudge-wink-wink.

I saw a thing I never thought I'd see –
In different coloured clothes, a man like me –
And now I understand that man's my brother;

But understanding just compounds the crime,
For now I hear the sergeant's call: It's time
To go back out and try to kill each other.

Ideas of March

sung to a Sousa beat

Shuffling off to Babylon to be born
again, in knife-sharp lines of infantry,
they march past tanks and massed artillery,
machinery themselves – No pause to mourn
the dead, to feel the baking heat or the dust,
which cakes itself in every liquid pore,
and blinds the eyes – Just marching onward – Just
the thought of vengeance to be theirs once more –
Eyes forward, not to note the weeping mother
by the burned hut, or spy the ragged children
who gather in gangs, whispering to one another,
"They killed my father; one day I will kill them" –
Forward they march to serve their country well,
to die again, and be reborn in hell.

Refugees

More than a mile the ragged line stretched out,
A mile of thin and dirty refugees
With here a limb gone, there an eye knocked out,
And everywhere starvation and disease;
More than a mile to a rusting khaki van
(Where soldiers handed out small bowls of rice)
To eat, and live another day, and then
Another day among the flies and lice.
The last one in the line was a small boy
With thin arms, holding out his hands for grain,
A meagre mouthful that would not bring joy
To him, or even still his stomach's pain.
    The rations finished – soldiers with no more –
    A small boy turned away – another war.

Evil

While loud the red-flecked mouths of cannons sing
And grapeshot whistles under empty sky;
While, red and green, before each preening King,
The massed battalions break, and thousands die;
While flowers bloom and sweet grass grows again
In splendid sunshine, under summer heat,
And madness grinds a hundred thousand men
Into a steaming pile of rotting meat . . .

A God smiles down through incense-laden air
At chalices and altars, gold, ornate,
And slowly dozes off to mumbled prayer
But wakes when black-clad mothers, bowed with grief
And weeping, clink into His silver plate
The few coins in a knotted handkerchief.

by Arthur Rimbaud
translated by George J. Dance

Mind Games

"What do you get from that epiphany?"
You like to ask. If I say I don't know:
"And if you knew, what would the answer be?"

"Why do you need a week alone to ski?"
You ask. I tell you I'm inspired by snow.
"What do you get from that? Epiphany?"

"I'm going to miss you. You know you'll miss me."
I don't know what to say (I have to go!)
And, if I knew, what would the answer be?

Enough! You pound on me persistently –
Though not to hurt me, just to crack ego.
(What do I get from that epiphany?)

I think you'll shatter me repeatedly
Till I surrender. But if I said so,
And if you knew, what would the answer be?

I redirect: "It isn't you, it's me –
I'm just not ready yet – Let's take it slow –"
What do we get from that epiphany,
And (if we knew) what would the answer be?

by Leisha Wharfield & George J. Dance

Prey

"Hello? Hello? Is anybody there?"
Silence, followed by a click and hum.
Slamming down, her lower arm goes numb.
She has to get outside; she needs some air.

The leaden sky leaks. Trees are gaunt and bare.
She walks – then runs – but every street has some
Eyes fondling her legs, her breasts, her bum,
And running filthy glances through her hair.

She's reached her block now – finally she nears
Her home, runs up the walk – inside once more,
Panting, trying to calm her breath and fears.

She's sure that bedroom door was closed before,
And weren't the lights on? What's that noise she
        hears?
How could she forget to lock the door?

My Pretty One

She took my pretty one away,
Left footprints on that precious clay,
She hurt him so, profaned his glory
But I've things to make her sorry:
Ropes to bind her in her place,
Acid for her sneering face,
Pliers and knives to pinch and cut,
Brands to burn the little slut,
Whips to make her skip and cry,
Needles sharp for either eye,
Matches and this gasoline
(Red blooms for the haughty queen),
Bullets for her dainty knees,
Germs to give her rare disease,
Bombs to make her fly in air
(Pieces here and pieces there) –
So many things to make you smile
And see I loved you all the while,
My pretty one. You'll know it's true
That everything was done for you.

Daily News

I don't want to look at the news today
But I don't want to talk (no, I'm not okay –
There's nothing to say – just go away)

So I stay head down in a corner booth
And I stare at the daily lies and truth
And I read: One charged in death of youth.

There's a picture of you, so fly, so cool,
So in control, so nobody's fool,
Big grin on your face, big idiot drool,

You hide beside your shyster guy
In a rented suit and a borrowed tie,
And I want to spit and I want to cry:

Badass motherfucker, hide behind your cool shades
– Cut a man for stepping on your blue suedes –
Fuck you, bitch, you ought to feel your own blades.

Better escape and run, boy, run
'Cause you had a knife, but I got a gun
And you fucked with me when you cut my son.

December

Entire city ablaze
with lights of every colour,
to stave off the black.

Whiteout

White flakes peeling
from a leprous sky.
Death is in the air.

The Woodsman

Oh, he had friends; and one soon brought the news
That all too soon the woodsman had to leave
His cabin, lakes, his forests, and his muse,
Abandoning the lot of them to grieve.
Yes, he had friends; but lived alone, remote,
Detesting much of modern life as tripe,
Within a world where living ghosts emote
Of cherry-blossomed boughs and cherry-ripe.
For forty years he sang among the pines,
He raged, he roared, he even raised the dead,
And does it still, in many thousand lines
That colours, had they been eyes, might have read;
    If colours had been eyes, they might have seen
    All that there was, and all there might have been.

The Sacred Candle

from Ambrose Bierce

Knowing that his time would soon be through,
The ill man bade his good wife to his side
To tell her: "Love, since we were groom and bride,
Until my hour of death, I have been true
And now, my dear, I pray the same of you.
Swear on this Sacred Candle here beside
My bed: So long as it shall be, you do
Not love again. Then I'll die satisfied."

She swore – they kissed – and soon he passed away,
His last view of this world being the sight of
His weeping wife, who tarried to attend
His cold and lifeless form till break of day,
Through blackest night relieved by just the light of
One candle, burning till the very end.

III Death

I

He told her that they had to leave at once,
that night he came home late from one more of
his brother's meetings for his brother's god
with those two men she'd never seen before.
They pointed to the seething mob outside
(at least a hundred yelling, holding signs
and throwing stones), declaring that they had
to go that very night, be gone by dawn
because the town was wicked, and their god
had stated that he would destroy it all.

Obediently, silently she packed
some things for her two youngest and herself.
Her older daughters and their husbands laughed
and told them they were crazy; that a god
does not just go around destroying towns.
He listened – hesitated – which enraged
the two in black, who suddenly began
to scream they had to leave right now, then grabbed
them, pulled them, almost dragged them out the back
into the waiting transport, and away.

II

Later she listened to his righteous snores
in a strange bed, and tried hard not to think
of everything she'd had to leave behind:
Her parents' graves – her daughters and their men
with children of their own now – her own home –
her sisters and her brothers – all her friends –
her neighbours who were there for every birth
and every illness – everyone she loved
but him (and did he even love her now?
It seemed he only loved his brother's god.)

By dawn she knew she had to go back home:
If it were true that god was going to
destroy the town, well, then she had to warn
them, didn't she? And if it were a lie,
then what exactly was she doing here?
Silently she left him to his snores,
awoke her daughters, warned them not to speak.
She dressed them quickly, quickly packed some
        things
then led them by the hand, without a sound,
away on foot upon the road to home.

III

The two in black caught up with her ten miles
outside of camp. They sent the daughters back
with him. They tied her up and dug a pit;
when it was deep enough, they threw her in
and buried her in sand up to her neck.
All morning she lay buried with the sun,
the red sun hammering, hammering on her head.
She begged them for some water, for a bit
of shade. She begged, she cursed, she even prayed
to their own god. They would not look at her.

They spent the next few hours gathering stones
methodically, without a word, to drop
them in a ring around her head. They paused
to pray to god in silence. Then, each one
picking up a stone, they cast it forth
and hit, bashed in the bone, and then again.
They stoned her for an hour. At the end,
when there was nothing left but sticky red,
they prayed again, then ate. Before they left,
they raised a cairn upon her broken skull.

IV

He didn't talk about it after that:
he heard in silence, turned aside to live,
raised children with his daughters, taught them well,
a faithful pillar of the true god's will
until the day he died. But once a year
he'd lead his daughters' children by the hand
a long way, to the shadow of the cairn,
in which he'd sit, one salt tear dropping down
upon the scorching sand, and tell the tale
of how their god had turned her into stone.

A Midwinter Night's Eve

No trace of summer yet; the earth was dead.
The sun was slowly dying, too, and like
Some ancient monarch lay, a rotting hulk
Wrapped in robes of pure magnificence –
Of purple, liquid gold, and bleeding red,
Reflecting off the scattered clouds above
Like flowers thrown upon a frozen grave.

A minute's silence for a fallen king.

The service over and the body lowered,
The very day now buried in the past,
With halting steps the widow turned away,
So painfully pulled on her cloak of black,
And hobbled off to seek oblivion
In dreams of reuniting with the sun.

Critique

The world no longer pours in through our eyes.
We cannot speak except of what we feel.
We do not know if anything is real,
Anything, or if it's all just lies.
These minds are dungeons, and we can't break free –
Caves from which we shall not be released –
Our only hope, to beg from some new priest
Some liberty in immortality.
No God above, no ground beneath our feet,
No books or poetry to save us now,
No what, no why, no where, no when, just how,
Each still must walk what seems to be a street,
   At best an ape with eyes that make it blind,
   Blundering through the dungeon of its mind.

Upanishad

What is the good of loving our desires
in this foul-smelling, insubstantial body
of bone, skin, muscle, marrow, semen, flesh,
tears, sweat, feces, urine, bile, and wind?

What is the good of loving our desires
when we can see the whole world is decaying,
when ants, mosquitoes, every living creature,
the very trees and rocks, arise and perish?

What is the good of loving our desires
when we can see the drying up of oceans,
the fall of mountains, and the earth's submergence,
even the disappearance of the stars?

What is the good of loving our desires?
Deliver me, and let me not exist.

New Year

after Tariq

Another year I think of auld lang syne.
Another day I visit with your stone.
Another night I shamble home to dine,
To drink and smoke, to read and sleep, alone.

I wish that I had rafters in my room.
I wish I had the guts to grab a noose,
 To feel my neck crack in the quiet gloom
And to be found tongue swollen, bowels loose.

January

black trees on white ground
with one fleck of colour,
a leaf unfallen

Threnody

When the clots of smoke that covered our earth like a
cerement
On the day we died, have thinned in the wind and
drifted
And the geese return across an azure sky,
Then somewhere below and beyond a broken horizon
From some yet unconquered green and golden island,
Resilient man will emerge, grow wise, and again read
What we have written in guilt, with an innocent eye.

Then, if the final song we shrieked like storm-cocks
At the first flash, outlives the ultimate thunder
To be misunderstood by quieter men,
Remember how we who dwelt in deepening shadow
(Dark over woodland, dark above cloud and water)
Looked upon beauty always as for the last time
And came to hate what we never would see again.

Remember how once we crushed the green bud,
uncertain
Of seeing the wind scatter red leaves in autumn,
Or broke the blue egg, that would never be born a
bird,
Or wondered, even, whether the white wave beating
Silently over the surface of the water
Should gain the distant shore of the sea in safety
Before we burned (our cries forever unheard).

I would speak with a boy as yet unborn, unburied,
Who has no threnody, yet, for the soon departed
In time of last light, awaiting eternal cold
(I know, yes, I know that millions of men before us
Have looked their last on all in the world that was
lovely
And perished as we now perish) and I would tell him:
"It should have been ours. We leave it to wrought and
mould."

In Violet Light

In violet light the fields are filled with snow,
Which drifts in blue-white wavelets, row by row.
Two icy burial mounds are heaped up high
Beside the road where walks a weary guy,
Lumbering home another mile or so.

From time to time a lone car crunches by,
But never stops, and leaves him with the cry
Of howling winds which never cease to blow
     In violet light,

The brutal winds that sting and stab each eye,
And whip his face until he, too, must cry.
His freezing body, numbed from foot to thigh,
Demanding he lie down a while to die,
He trudges on: Just one more mile to go
     In violet light.

Logos

I. Liturgy

In the beginning, I remember
Turning to you in darkness
In the void,
Your body without form
A darker mist beside me
And how there was no sin

How in the gloom your silhouette
grew an arm to hold
the black, to push it back,
How then there was light
And we could see

And, not seeing, could sense
The staccato
Of rain above, the bass
Of nearby falls, and beyond,
Forever swelling,
The pulse of the ocean ...

The way I dropped
as into sweet grass
in a clearing beneath
cathedral pines thrusting,
to taste each berry,

To breathe every flower,
To sink as into living green to bleed

And how with the blood
Came the animal rising,
Standing, massing, chanting,
Pounding on the skin drum
Harder, my love, ever harder
My love
And how that was creation
And how that was new life
And how that was sin

And how there will again
Be sin tomorrow
The day of the dead god
Tomorrow, when you turn away
In silence and walk past
Tomorrow, when we will both feel torn
for a word we could not find

But for now you rest.

II. Oblation

"How
Could it be, a mere braincase
Knows anything of time and space?"
The darkness hovers, nearer now.
"How could a mind
Shine any light
On what no eye
Can ever see?"

The tide thrusts high
The swelling ocean,
Waves reach
Up invitingly
And the night
Spits an answer back:
"Wrap yourself in a public myth,
Stay blind
To how your thought is free –"
"– or drown yourself!" adds the glistening black
That slaps with
A dead hand on the beach;
A motion
That no living hand
Can grasp, no mind can understand. .

III. Consecration

To watch the stillness in moving things;
Light, rock, water over rock,
How they have emerged from nothing;
To see the future tensed
Within a seed, a mind
the motion within the still;
To build and, building, rise
Creating from such nothing
The building rising from the rock,
Power from water bearing light;
To write in poems of carbon
Rising from mind the word –
    "Deus, ecce deus"
– the way these all emerge from nothing,
Permanence from void, the logos
Still within – now and forever
Movement and stillness
Ascending the spiral,
Climbing the ancient winding stair
The fixed point always present, always still
Within the ascent;
It is of such things
That our myths are made:

IV. Communion

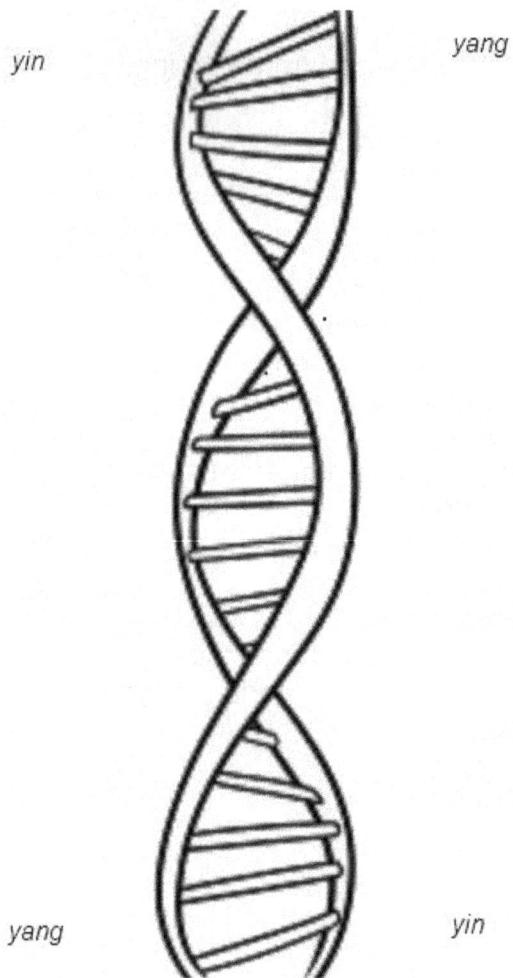

yin   yang

yang   yin

V. Benediction

Nothing was changed by the risen sun
Itself, yet all is enlightened since darkness fled:
The land behind me skull-white to be green,
Ahead grey ocean to be vivid aqua,
All at rest, all in motion, all of it
Particles in random chaos
Become molecules in rigid stasis,
So much from void; my eyes the very same
Giving it all the beauty,
My words the meaning,
My hearing the song. I am
The hub, the fixed point,
The still point without which there is no dance
And there is always the dance,
Movement and stillness ever entwined,
Now illuminated. Yet
Nothing is changed, no, nothing is new
But a new light over the sea; while on the sea
Another ship charts course, churning
Blades into spume, shearing
Prow through breakers, curling
Sheets of white water
Around the mewing gulls.

February

Unnoticed dreams:
Ocean waves in winter,
The curve of your cheek.

Winter Love

Most anyone could fall in love
  When spring is in the breeze,
When sun bakes down and pungent sap
  Pours through the veins and trees;

But love that lasts through freezing blasts
  Is rare beyond a price.
How beautiful when love endures
  Preserved in snow and ice.

Afterglow

My darling, on this night of Valentine's,
Excuse me while I find a way to say
I love you, knowing I could never pay
For thirty years with only fourteen lines.
But let me try to say just what I mean:
That in the depths of February's chill,
As long as I can have you with me still,
It never will be dark or cold, Maureen;
For, holding you and looking at the snow,
    I see a light from thirty years ago
Still blazing, gleaming, dazzling all below!
And looking in your eyes, Maureen, I know
    A passion from as many years ago,
Which warms my body with its afterglow.

There Was a Time

There was a time my love and I
Would lie upon the summer grass,
To watch the white clouds wander by
In heaven, and their shadows pass.

The sun poured down like honey then,
The breezes cooled like morning dew,
And life was more magnificent
Than either of us ever knew.

My love was once like sparkling wine
And now she tastes of wholesome bread,
Her flavours faded – so have mine –
But we are both completely fed.

It's quite enough that she is here
Beside me every hour and day,
But more than that, each passing year,
There's time to take my love away

Into a meadow, where we'll lie
Together on the summer grass,
To watch the white clouds wander by
In heaven, and the shadows pass.

God Be With You

You tell me that you're leaving me today.
You've met the man you want; he wants you, too.
He's taking you, not far but still, away,
And I'm afraid there's nothing I can do.

That's what I get for trying to love two:
You need a greater passion in your life,
As strong and pure as that which comes from you,
The kind that he will show to you, his wife;

So go, my daughter, go to your new man.
I still can love you; you will still love me.
I'll be there for you, as and when I can,
To find, in time, that I am loving three,

And I am sure I'll soon be loving four:
Love opens arms to bring in more, and more.

Possibilities

So many possibilities
Begin with every baby's birth,
But years conspire to decrease
So many possibilities.
Yet still we have our families
To justify our time on earth;
So many possibilities
Begin with every baby's birth.

Small Steps

With picks on shoulders, headlamps beaming light,
We take another step towards the dark.
Black walls to either side obstruct our sight
As we pace slowly forward bearing light
In silence: No canaries sing tonight.

We sometimes stumble, sometimes leave a mark
Or find a gem while following our light,
Advancing step by step into the dark.

Long May You Live

Long may you live, long after I am gone,
And may you always fix your thoughts upon
Our memories; may the good times you and I
Enjoyed be points of light to journey by,
Like fireflies upon a twilit lawn.

May each day find you welcoming the dawn
And living life complete: each day to try,
To win, to celebrate with your head high.
        Long may you live.

May you walk in righteousness through Babylon,
True to yourself, not anybody's pawn;
And on that far-off day when you must die,
Once more may you remember me, and sigh,
And leave one wish for those who carry on:
        "Long may you live."

Index of first lines

www.ingramcontent.com/pod-product-compliance
Lightning Source LLC
Chambersburg PA
CBHW022341040426
42449CB00006B/660